HEROES AND WARRIORS

El Cid

CHAMPION OF SPAIN

JOHN MATTHEWS
Plates by JAMES FIELD

Firebird Books

For Wolfe, Johan, Rhiannon and Imogen Van Brussel

Acknowledgements

No work on El Cid could possibly be undertaken without the scholarship of Ramon Pidal, to whose tireless efforts in unearthing the real figure of El Cid the present author owes an immeasurable debt. To my wife Caitlín, who kept me fuelled with advice, love and cups of coffee, and who typed much of the manuscript from my unreadable scrawl, thanks are not enough. Without her I would still be struggling. Finally, thanks to the Spanish National Tourist Board in London for permission to reproduce their photographs.

J.M.

First published in the UK 1988 by Firebird Books
P.O. Box 327, Poole, Dorset BH15 2RG

Copyright © 1988 Firebird Books Ltd
Text copyright © 1988 John Matthews

Distributed in the United States by
Sterling Publishing Co, Inc,
2 Park Avenue, New York, NY 10016

Distributed in Australia by
Capricorn Link (Australia) Pty Ltd
PO Box 665, Lane Cove, NSW 2066

British Library Cataloguing in Publication Data

Matthews, John, *1948–*
El Cid: champion of Spain —— (Heroes and warriors).
1. Cid   2. Heroes —— Spain
Biography
I. Title   II. Field, James   III. Series
942.03′2′0924   DA207

ISBN 1 85314 004 X

Series editor Stuart Booth
Designed by Kathryn S.A. Booth
Typeset by Inforum Limited, Portsmouth
Colour separations by Kingfisher Facsimile
Colour printed by Riverside Printing Co (Reading) Ltd
Printed and bound in Great Britain at the Bath Press

El Cid

CHAMPION OF SPAIN

THE SPAIN OF EL CID

DUCHIES OF
AQUITAINE
AND POITIERS

THE FRANKS

Santiago ASTURIAS •Oviedo

GALICIA

Kingdom of
Navarre and Aragon
(Sancho Ramires)

•Leon Bivar •

Kingdom of Leon and Castille
(Alfonso VI)

•Burgos

**Kingdom of
Saragossa**
(Mostain 1085–1101
El Cid 1081–87)

PORTUGAL Zamora •

CHRISTIAN SPAIN

•Segovia

Salamanca •

Toledo •

Kingdom of Badajoz
(Omar Motawakkil)

MOSLEM SPAIN

Kingdom of Seville
(Ben Abbed Motamid)

Kingdom of Granada
(Abdallah)

•Granada

• Gibraltar
Ceuta

Tangier •

*With a trampling of drenched, red hoofs
and an earthquake of men that meet,
strong war sets hand to the scythe, and
the furrows take fire from his feet.*
(*Erectheus* Swinburne)

El Cid Campeador – Rodrigo del Bivar

He was Rodrigo del Bivar – otherwise known as El Cid or 'the Lord' – one of the most complex and remarkable heroes of the Middle Ages. In his most familiar guise, as a literary figure, he is brave, heroic, loyal, a good husband and father, a redoubtable foe and a man of honour. In short, he is all that a medieval paladin might be expected to be. However, even within that most famous and partisan account of his life, the twelfth century *Poema del Cid*, there is an element of cunning, almost knavish behaviour which is far from usual in such a character. El Cid lies, cheats, even steals from innocent men; while elsewhere the portrait is even less flattering.

Yet despite all this, El Cid is probably Spain's greatest hero. He is famed for his just behaviour, nobility and magnanimity. He was so respected by his natural enemies, the Moors, that when he was exiled by his Christian overlords, they were more than willing to give him shelter and employment. Indeed, it was the Moors who gave him the title by which he is best known, a contraction of the Arabic *sid-y*, meaning 'my lord'.

He was born in 1043 at Bivar, a village to the north of Burgos in northern Spain. As the son of noble parents, Rodrigo was brought up and trained in knightly pursuits at the court of Prince Sancho, eldest son of King Ferdinand of Castile and Leon. He soon proved himself a redoubtable warrior, and won the respect of his peers. When, with the death of Ferdinand in 1065, civil war broke out between his surviving sons, Rodrigo commanded the army of his overlord Prince Sancho.

Then, in 1077, Sancho was murdered and El Cid became a favourite at the court of his brother Alfonso and his sister Urraca. There was believed to have been an incestuous relationship between Alfonso and Urraca and they were probably responsible for Sancho's death. Whether or not he suspected this, Rodrigo accepted the favours bestowed upon him by the new King – including marriage to Alfonso's niece Ximena Diaz.

It seems to have been a happy marriage and Ximena bore Rodrigo two daughters. But Rodrigo had made many enemies, both among the disgraced followers of the murdered Sancho (who saw his change of

5

Warriors of El Cid's time, in mail shirts; from an eleventh century ivory reliquary of San Millan de la Copolla.

allegiancies as disaster) and those at the court of Alfonso (who saw his rise as a threat). In particular, the powerful Beni-Gomez family schemed continually against Rodrigo until Alfonso banished him in 1081.

It was from this point that Rodrigo's life as a wandering and heroic adventurer began in earnest. He gathered a considerable following of loyal and disaffected men, and together they served many masters, both Christian and Moslem, during the next five years.

Then, in 1095, a new influx of Moorish invaders landed in Spain. They were led by a fanatical chieftain named Yusuf and Alfonso was soundly defeated at the battle of Sagrajas. Rodrigo, by now widely known as El Cid Campeador (the battler), was recalled to favour and proceeded at once to drive back the invaders. This he did with such success that within the next few years his name became a byword throughout Spain.

From then until his death in 1099 at the age of fifty-six, El Cid fought a series of dazzling campaigns against the Moors, taking the fortified city of Valencia and making it an impregnable fortress against his enemies When news of his death reached the rest of Spain, men and women wept openly in the streets, tearing their clothing and lacerating their cheeks in an extravagent display of mourning.

Many refused to believe El Cid was actually dead. Just as with other heroes like Arthur and Charlemagne, it was thought that he had been transported to another time or place to await his country's greatest need. The legend of El Cid began there, but nearly a thousand years were to pass before the true story of his life and deeds began to be known.

Valley of Sajambre, near Leon (opposite). Rodrigo was born near here at Bivar in 1043 and would have spent much of his childhood in sight of these rugged hills.

Eleventh Century Spain

El Cid was born into a world of complex, shifting forces and allegiances, both religious and political. Indeed, the situation changed so swiftly that

there is almost no resemblance between the political maps of Spain for 1000 and 1050, or again between those covering the times of the birth and death of El Cid.

For much of this time the country was in a continual state of war, with the Moors in the south and the Christians in the north constantly invading each others' borders. However, there was never any clear dividing line between north and south, neither culturally nor physically. Despite a veneer of Islamicism, many of the Spanish Moslems were originally of Gothic or Iberio–Roman stock. They were separated from their northern neighbours only by religious beliefs. Furthermore, since at this time Islam was pursuing a policy of particular openness towards other religions, less of a barrier existed than is sometimes assumed. Indeed, there was such a degree of integration between the two that even modern Spain retains a powerful element of Orientalism within its cultural makeup.

Moorish Spain came into being over a period of several hundred years – from the period of the first Moslem conquest in the eighth century, to the eventual re-conquest by Christians from the north of the peninsula in the later part of the thirteenth century. In the interim there existed a period of extraordinary cross-fertilization between Christian and Arabic cultures. In the words of the historian Pierre Vilar:

Moorish Spain was in fact a crucible in which were fused the contributions of diverse cultures . . . The products of this crucible filter across Christian Europe – scholastic philosophy, romanesque art, the school of medicine at Montpelier, the lyric poetry of the troubadours and the mystical poetry of Dante.

(*Spain: A Brief History*)

This interaction occurred because of the very fragmentation experienced by the country. After the breakdown of the Omyniad caliphates under Al-Mansur around 1030, Spain became a patchwork of small communities and states. Each claimed a king – or even, in one case, an emperor – and they included the purely Christian, the Moslem-influenced, the purely Moorish, and the Christian-influenced Islamicism. It was an extraordinarily fluid ratio of exchange which would be hard to parallel today. Perhaps a graphic parallel would be to imagine that a country existed in the middle of Europe which was at one and the same time Catholic, Protestant, Jewish and Islamic, while sharing equally the cultural and economic influence of the USA, USSR, and China!

At this time, the Christian factions within the Caliphates (ex-slaves and captives who had risen to high office under Al-Mansur) requested help from the Court of Castile. This was an extraordinary state of affairs but one which enabled Rodrigo del Bivar to serve so many masters without apparent conflict. It is also the reason why he could lay claim to a rich blend of cultures, having an excellent grasp of the European legal system and Arabic poetry and customs. This was reflected too in dress that combined Moorish robes with European mail and weaponry.

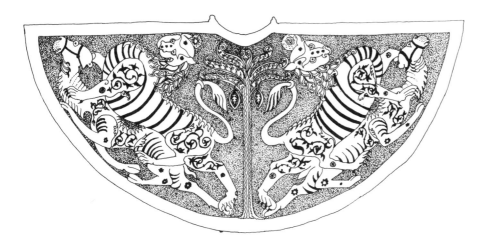

The length of time during which the frontiers of the Christian and Moorish regions continued to shift, meant that there was ample opportunity for cultural and religious exchange. There seems to have existed a form of Spanish Islam which was like nothing then available anywhere in Europe. When they were not fighting each other, the kings and caliphs were just as likely to be seeking each other's protection or vasalage. Thus, while these enlightened times continued, there existed little of the prejudice and fanaticism which were engendered by the Crusades.

Gold embroidered cape showing the influence of Moorish art in the design of lions attacking camels. Such a garment may well have been worn by Alfonso III for his coronation.

Mix of Cultures

The cultural achievements of the Moors in Spain far outstripped those of the semi-barbarian north. Philosophy, medicine and the arts flourished in an enlightened atmosphere which existed scarcely anywhere else at the time. Moktadir and Mutamin, two of the Moslem lords with whom El Cid took service during his years of exile, were themselves scholars and poets of no small skill. Rodrigo must have learned a great deal from these intelligent, cultured people. Certainly his years with the Moors seem to have changed him, softening without blunting his warlike character.

In cities such as Toledo, which was reconquered by the Christian forces in 1085, an even more extraordinary mix of philosophies and beliefs obtained in something approaching harmony. A strong Jewish faction introduced the roots of the mystical system known as Qabalism. Similarly, there were practitioners, among both Moslem and Christian, of the 'hermetic arts' of alchemy, science and mystical theology.

In the north of Spain, on the other hand, there was a dearth of learning and an almost total disregard for the arts – except where Moorish influence was most strongly felt. Philosophy was frowned upon as almost certainly heretical, while the Catholic Church generally strove to outlaw even classical learning in favour of theological treatises.

There arose therefore an interesting situation. The Christian Spanish had looked towards their Moslem neighbours as arbiters of culture and

9

learning. Yet, when faced once again with war between north and south, Christian and Moor, they found themselves unable to relate to their brothers in France or Italy, who in turn regarded them as scandalously Islamicised. As Ramon Pidal puts it:

By the eleventh century, Al Andalus was populated by an extremely heterogeneous mass, part of which was still Christian whilst another part was only half Moslem.

Political maps of the time show how complex the situation really was when Rodrigo began to exercise an influence. From the eighth century onward, there was a strong Christian presence in the northerly mountainous regions of Asturias, Cantabria and Galicia; while in the south the caliphates flourished in Cordoba, Seville, Toledo and Granada. Between these two, an unequivocal dividing line made the plateaux of Leon and Burgos a kind of no-mans-land, across which the two forces ranged more or less in a continual dispute until the middle of the tenth century. Then the forces of the Asturian kings pushed further south, founding states in Leon, Castile and Burgos. It is the fates of these kingdoms which form the background of El Cid's area of greatest activity. Had he never existed, it is probable that the Almoravid Moors, under their fanatical leader Yusuf, would have overrun a far greater area of central Spain – and perhaps prevented the gradual blurring of the two cultures which produced the later kingdoms of Moorish Spain and thereafter the great empire of the sixteenth century.

Arms and Battle Tactics

Two things gave the Christian forces in Spain superiority over their Moslem foes: the weight of their armour and horses, and their possession of massive siege engines. Castile itself had been named after the fortresses

The mangonel, which projected massive, damaging boulders and was a vital engine of siege warfare for the Christian forces.

built along the border between Christian and Moslem Spain, and essentially those who held these castles held the greatest degree of control over the lands on either side. For this reason, the great part of reports relating to warfare in this period concern sieges. We hear endlessly of Rodrigo taking various fortified cities and castles – only to lose them later and often in a matter of months.

By this time, the Christians had virtually perfected the art of siege warfare, using the powerful mangonel, among other massive siege engines. This machine could project massive boulders against the walls of a besieged castle with the power of a cannon. Similarly, the trebuchet could lob the lifeless carcass of a horse (or more often a human corpse) over the walls, to add to the disease already raging within.

The Moors depended more on starvation tactics and in sheer weight of numbers; they scarcely ever adapted to the use of siege towers or other engines of war, until the widespread use of cannon and gunpowder several centuries later.

However, on open ground, the Moors' skill as horsemen and the magnificent Arab steeds they rode, gave them a positive advantage over the heavily armoured war-horses of the Christians, which were more like carthorses, slow and heavy against the speedy, light Arab mounts.

The Moslems also wore much lighter armour and carried light swords, bows and spears. Again, these gave them the advantage when it came to the swift 'attack-and-run' tactics which they frequently employed. The heart-shaped shields of the Moslems, called *adarga*, proved so popular that they were sometimes adopted by their opponents.

The great castle of Montellana–Coronil in Seville. It saw much of the fighting between Moors and Christians during El Cid's lifetime.

However, in a head-on clash, the weight and armour-piercing qualities of the Christian forces were virtually unstoppable.

Nonetheless, the cost of maintaining a fully armoured force was considerable; hence the frequent failure of kings like Alfonso to raise sufficiently large forces. Weapons and armour, measured in the equivalent of cows, have been quoted as being worth as much as:

Helmet *6 cows*
Mail-coat *12 cows*
Sword and scabbard *7 cows*
Leg armour *6 cows*
Lance and shield *2 cows*
Horse *12 cows*

Both sides made use of bows, though the Moslems were by far the more proficient in their use. In hand-to-hand fighting, once again the huge and heavy broad-swords of the Christians proved superior over the light, curved scimitars of their adversaries. Again, in the use of spears, the Christian knight, crouched behind his kite-shaped shield, atop his massive war horse could topple a lightly armed man completely out of the saddle – and probably spear him through in the process.

All of these qualities, when duly accounted for, amounted to a virtual condition of stalemate between the opposing forces. The almost weekly loss and gain of territory depended entirely on the skills of leadership and prevailing conditions. In a straight fight, the Christians usually won; in skirmishes, the Moslem forces held their own and often overcame their opponents with fanatical zeal.

Moorish infantry and cavalry, armed with bows, swords and spears, and carrying small round shields.

12

The Courts of Leon and Castile

Ferdinand I of Castile and Leon was crowned on 21st June 1038. He was a strong and greedy monarch who pursued a course of military aggrandisement from the very beginning of his reign. He desired to subjugate the whole of Moslem Spain and to integrate this vast tract of land into his own kingdom, which would then be the single greatest state in the country. So confident was he of his success that he assumed the title

Three warriors of about 1150, wearing conical helms and long mail shirts and carrying kite-shaped shields. Armed with spears and swords they reflect the style of Rodrigo's army.

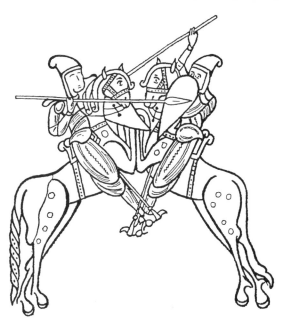

Knights battling, from an eleventh century Spanish manuscript.

'Emperor' while his plans were still far from completion. However, his great energy and militaristic abilities enabled him to extend his sway deep into Moorish territory – in particular the Caliphate of Valencia. By 1065 he had conquered Toledo and made it a Christian–Moorish fief owing allegiance to Leon. He was on the point of taking the key fortress of Valencia in the same year, when he fell sick and died within a matter of weeks. His realm was split between his three sons Sancho, Alfonso and Garcia, along the lines of a will he had made in 1063.

To his second, favourite son Alfonso, he gave the Kingdom of Leon and the Campos Goticos, together with the tributes from the Moorish kingdom of Toledo, whose overlord he had successfully beaten into submission only a year before. To Sancho, his first-born, he gave the smaller inheritance of Castile and the tribute of Saragossa. Garcia, the third son, received Galicia and Portugal, along with the tribute of Badajar and Seville. To his daughters, Urraca and Elvira, he gave dominion over all the monasteries within his borders, on the sole understanding that they did not marry and thereby produce alternate heirs to the kingdom.

On hearing of these terms and before Ferdinand died, Sancho refused to accept this partition on the grounds that it went against the rights of the eldest son. It is said that Ferdinand made all three brothers promise to defer to Rodrigo del Bivar, putting him virtually *in loco parentis* to the *infantas*, though he was still only of an age with them.

So, with the death of Ferdinand all was quiet for a time. Sancho, ruling in Castile, at once began to extend his territories, assisted by Rodrigo, who was given the title of Ensign, a position which automatically gave him command of the army.

14

El Cid's Early Adventures

One of Rodrigo's earliest exploits was his win in a single combat against the champion of Navarre in order to settle a border dispute between Sancho and the Navarran king. Soon after, in 1067, he lead the armies of Castile against the Moorish city of Saragossa, subduing it effectively and extracting a firm promise of fealty and prompt payment of tribute. A Jewish chronicler attributed the success of the expedition entirely to the youthful Ensign, calling him for the first time 'Cidi', the equivalent of *Mio Cid* 'my lord'.

Then, in 1067, Ferdinand's widow died, thus removing any scruple remaining in the mind of Sancho towards honouring the partition. Within a year, Castile was at war with Leon, brother against brother. As always, Rodrigo del Bivar was in the forefront of the action.

The first action in the brief war was the battle of Llantada Plain on 19th July 1068. Castile was the victor, but instead of surrendering himself, as had previously been agreed, Alfonso fled south. Gathering his forces, he attacked the Moorish state of Badajoz, evincing a still higher tribute than was already paid to the third brother Garcia.

The result was a further outbreak of hostilities between the three sons of Ferdinand, with Sancho pretending to side with Garcia against Alfonso, while really waiting his moment to annex Galicia and Portugal.

Ramon Pidal gives a rounded portrait of the brothers at this time:

Garcia of Galicia lacked the ability possessed by his brothers and accordingly was the first victim of the discord among them all. Sancho was ambitious, headstrong, and overbearing and was noted for his indomitable courage . . . Alfonso, on the other hand, though go-ahead and energetic, was of a docile nature and readily deferred to his parents and his eldest sister Urraca, so that he became the favourite son and developed all the traits of a spoilt child.

Whether El Cid acted in a position of arbiter, as Ferdinand had intended, is not known; he seems to have stepped aside from the almost continuous wrangling of the brothers. In 1071, this conflict resulted in the capture and exile of Garcia and the subsequent division of his lands between Sancho and Alfonso. Some of the near contemporary songs which have survived from the period describe Rodrigo himself as capturing Garcia and handing him over to the brothers. It may be that he saw this as the best means of curtailing a war that was tearing apart Christian Spain.

With Garcia effectively out of the running, relations between Sancho and Alfonso worsened. Several border engagements took place, culminating in the battle of Golpejera. Here Sancho was heard to remark that he was the equal of a thousand men while Rodrigo was equal to another hundred. El Cid replied, modestly, that he was only equal to one man at a time, and that as for the rest it was up to God. However, in the battle which followed it was certainly Rodrigo who helped turn the tide of events for Sancho. Alfonso was taken prisoner, possibly by El Cid himself, and subsequently exiled to Toledo. With him went several

The Gateway of San Andres, Zamora. The city saw much conflict during El Cid's campaigns, as the ebb and flow of conquest and recovery gave it first a Christian master and then a Moorish one. It may have changed hands as often as eight times in a period of twenty years.

members of the Beni-Gomez family, and it is from this that their hatred of Rodrigo dates.

Sancho meanwhile had himself crowned king of Leon, and thus came to rule over the most extensive kingdom in the whole of Christian Spain.

However, his success was to be short-lived. His sister Urraca, who was believed to harbour an elicit passion for Alfonso, raised a rebellion against Sancho. When he arrived outside her castle of Zamora, she sent a man into the royal camp to murder him. Sancho fell dying outside his own pavilion while Rodrigo and others gave chase. However, the assassin escaped back to Zamora, which opened its gates to him.

Sancho's death at the age of 34 struck fear into the hearts of his followers, many of whom fled. Only Rodrigo was able to rally enough men to escort the King's body to its resting place in the monastery of Ona.

Urraca at once sent messengers to Alfonso who, having won the support of the Moorish king of Toledo, left his place of exile to proclaim himself King of Castile, Leon and Galicia. At the same time he proclaimed Urraca as Queen, giving her the status she would normally have attained if she were actually his consort.

But not all the lords of the kingdoms supported Alfonso. Rodrigo del Bivar was one who did not. Indeed, in a remarkable episode, El Cid is said to have forced Alfonso to swear an oath on sacred relics to the effect

El Cid leads his heavily-armed and mounted soldiers in a desperate foray from the besieged fortress of Valencia. The sheer weight and ferocity of their charge carries them through the massed ranks of their Moorish adversaries.

that he had nothing to do with his brother's murder. In this, Rodrigo once again displayed his judgement of what was best for Spain, for under this oath Alfonso gained the support of those who doubted his right to rule, as well as the support of El Cid himself, who now showed himself willing to stand by the new King.

Alfonso took the oath, but he never forgave Rodrigo for forcing him to humble himself before the rest of his vassals.

Status, Marriage and Banishment

El Cid now became an honoured member of Alfonso's court – but he no longer held the high office of Ensign as he had during Sancho's reign. Also his foes, the Beni-Gomez family, and in particular Garcia Ordonez, began a rise to power almost in equal measure to the decline of El Cid.

Meanwhile, the fate of the unfortunate Garcia was now sealed. On the advice of his sister, Alfonso summoned his youngest and only surviving brother who, expecting to be restored to his throne, came willingly. He was immediately seized and thrown into prison, where he remained in chains for a further seventeen years, finally falling sick and dying before a suddenly contrite Alfonso could order his chains removed. Garcia's epitaph, written by a monk of Leon, made clear the opinion of the time:

Here lies Garcia, King of Galicia and Portugal, taken captive by his brother's craft. He died in chains on 22nd March, 1090.

In 1074 Alfonso surprisingly arranged an excellent marriage for El Cid with his own niece Donna Ximena Diaz. By all accounts she was something of a beauty. Also, being of royal descent from the House of Aragon, her marriage not only demonstrated to all that Rodrigo stood in high favour with the King, but also helped heal the breach between Castile and Leon. Ximena was seen as representing the former, while Rodrigo, who had formally renounced his rights as a Castilian noble, now stood for Leon.

Thus, for a time, Rodrigo's fortunes were restored. But gradually the Beni-Gomez family worked on the mind of Alfonso. They reminded him of the ignominious episode of the oath-taking, and pointed out that Rodrigo now had a personal 'army' almost as large as the King's. Matters came to a head when Rodrigo lead his men against a revolt of both Christians and Moors at Toledo, a revolt in which the Beni–Gomez family were certainly involved. Diego Ordonez lost no time in accusing El Cid of seeking to further his own ends by laying claim to Toledo, something which Rodrigo never appears to have intended.

The outcome was that Alfonso banished his most trusted vassal, giving him ten days to leave Castile and Leon.

Bestowing his wife and children in the safety of the monastery at Cardena, Rodrigo departed to his exile. However, his departure was more like triumph since he took with him some 2000 men who preferred

El Cid upholds his honour and that of his King by defeating an enemy champion in single combat. Having unhorsed each other, the two men finish the fight on foot, in a hand-to-hand trial of strength.

to go into exile with him rather than remain in Alfonso's service. The next few years were to establish Rodrigo as one of the truly remarkable soldiers of his time. They were to be wandering years, but they were to end in triumph.

Exile and the Peril out of Africa

The normal recourse of exiled Spanish knights was to the nearest Moorish court, but Rodrigo made instead for the Kingdom of Barcelona. There he attempted to persuade the counts Ramon and Berenguer to aid him in taking Saragossa, a key fortress which King Ferdinand had long sought to bring under his sway.

Rodrigo met with a cold and scornful reception from the counts, who believed they had no need of a renegade knight with a rather large force of his own. So he took an extraordinary step, going directly to Moktadir, the Moslem ruler of Saragossa, and pledging his sword and men to the Moorish prince. Moktadir, who was seriously threatened by the neighbouring kingdoms of Navarre and Aragon, gladly accepted. When he died shortly after the arrival of El Cid, his son Motamid ratified the agreement and honoured Rodrigo by placing him in joint command of the army.

Rodrigo and Motamid rapidly began to make inroads into the border territory separating the Caliphates of Saragossa and Lerida. The latter was in the hands of Motamid's younger brother, who at once made an alliance with most of the states of Catalonia, including Barcelona, where El Cid had recently offered his services and been turned away.

It was the same story over again, brother against brother, neighbour against neighbour; and as before Rodrigo was caught in the middle. Nevertheless, he quickly captured Count Berenger and slaughtered most of his followers when he overwhelmed their camp outside the city of Tamarinte. Upon his return to Saragossa, El Cid was treated as a hero in exactly the same way as if he had been a Moslem. Motamid heaped gifts upon him, gold and jewels and rich silks. But Rodrigo was not like other mercenaries; he made it clear that he required nothing for himself. Instead, he negotiated an unofficial treaty which made Saragossa subject to Castile and Leon, and established the Caliphate as a virtual protectorate of Alfonso's kingdom.

There then followed an episode which further proved Cid's loyalty and Alfonso's treacherous nature. The Emperor – as he was by then styling himself – led an attack on a castle close to the border of Saragossa. In the event, he was defeated and fled after the death of most of his forces. Rodrigo, hearing of this, rushed to Alfonso's aid and for a moment it seemed that the Emperor would relent and rescind El Cid's banishment.

However, though Rodrigo was willing to give up his exalted position at Saragossa, Alfonso regained his nerve and at once again turned against his ally – and El Cid returned to Saragossa.

Alfonso entered a period of personal success which nearly eclipsed El Cid for some two years. Then, in the winter of 1085, Alfonso arrived at the gates of Saragossa and laid siege to the city. Rodrigo, who was elsewhere at the time, heard the news with dismay. His honour would not permit him to attack his sovereign, yet he still owed allegiance to Motamid.

He chose to do nothing, and for a time remained in a distant castle as a virtual prisoner of conscience.

Alfonso pressed forward on all fronts. After a heavy assault, he took the great city of Toledo which became his chief fortress on the eastern frontier, extending his kingdom still further into Moorish territory. Many of the Moslem kings now came forward with tributes and it seemed, briefly, that most of Moorish Spain was about to fall to the Christians. This would indeed have made it one of the greatest empires in Europe. But two men prevented this, one indirectly, the other by force of arms: Rodrigo del Bivar and the Almoravid chieftain, Yusuf ibn Teshufin.

The Almoravids were really Berbers from the region of the Sahara. In the eleventh century, they were one of two nomadic tribes to erupt into sudden and ferocious activity, for at the other end of the Mediterranean, the Seljuk Turks poured into Asia Minor.

The Almoravids swiftly overran much of Africa and the Sudan, restoring these countries to orthodox Islamic practice. This they administered with sword and fire, destroying taverns and burning musical instruments as symbols of moral corruption.

It was to these fanatical warriors, and above all to their chieftain, that both Motamid and the Caliph of Badajoz appealed for aid against the steady encroachments of Alfonso. Having twice refused on the grounds that he had first to win Tangier and Ceuta (which he accomplished in 1084), Yusuf finally turned his attention to Spain at Motamid's third desperate request.

He landed, with a vast army, on 30th June 1086 and was met by Motamid and the Moslem Kings of Granada and Malaga at the head of their own forces.

Alfonso, hearing the news, at once raised the siege of Saragossa and began to assemble his own forces. The two armies met at Sagrajas and the first to engage with the Christians were Motamid's own native Spanish Moslems. Yusuf held back, coolly remarking that both sides were their enemies and that the more they slaughtered each other the better.

Finally, Yusuf advanced and the thunderous roll of the Moorish

The royal bodyguard of King Alfonso III (866–909) armed with swords, lances and shields, both round and kite-shaped.

19

drums was heard for the first time on Spanish soil. The compact, organized attack of the Moors shook the Christians; they were more used to single combats where the actions of one man could turn the day. The disciplined ranks of the Almoravid army inflicted terrible losses. They were more lightly armed than Alfonso's knights, but their new way of fighting turned the scales in their favour.

Finally, Yusuf led into the fray his own Black Guards, consisting of 4000 men. Armed with light Indian swords and shields of hippopotamus hide, they fought their way through to the King, forcing him to withdraw, wounded in the thigh.

At the end of the day, Alfonso escaped with barely 500 men, most of whom were wounded. Meanwhile Yusuf caused the heads of the slain to be cut off and piled in heaps, from the top of which his muezzins called the faithful to prayer.

Now, at last, Alfonso called out to El Cid to come to his aid. He sent waggon-loads of treasure and a great entourage of knights to Saragossa with requests for a formal reconciliation. In effect, he need not have bothered; he had only to ask in the name of Spain and Rodrigo would have come.

The two men met in Toledo in the spring of 1087 and with the exception of El Cid's old enemies, there was general rejoicing from those who believed that if Rodrigo had commanded the army at Sagrajas the outcome would have been different.

Yusuf, meanwhile, much to everyone's astonishment, returned to Africa, having learned of the death of his son. He left only a token force of 3000 horsemen under the command of Motamid.

Spanish Christendom thus enjoyed a respite and Alfonso lost no time in consolidating his battered forces. The losses at the Battle of Sagrajas had been great and not even the addition of El Cid's men could make it anything like as strong as it had been before the coming of Yusuf.

However, Rodrigo was disinclined to sit behind the walls of Saragossa. He set about raising an army of his own to win back the lands lost in the recent campaign. Many men, elated at the prospect of fighting under El Cid, flocked to him.

With a force totalling some 7000, he began to subdue much of eastern Castile, making it as strong as it had been before Sagrajas. He also succeeded in winning pledges from the rulers of Valencia, then perhaps the most prized city of Spain.

This astonishing success, considering the size of his forces and the difficulty of much of the terrain over which he fought, only succeeded in outraging Alfonso, who seems to have believed – or been persuaded to believe – that El Cid intended to set up a rival kingdom in Valencia. However, before the King's unjust rage had time to ripen, news came that Yusuf had returned and was marching north. Alfonso at once set out to meet him, sending a peremptory command to Rodrigo to join him.

Somehow, in the confusion of rapid troop movements, El Cid never succeeded in joining with the royal army, though he certainly attempted to do so. Yusuf, who had returned with a smaller force than before and doubted the strength of his Spanish allies, abruptly withdrew. Alfonso was victorious without striking a blow; and his anger at the failure of El Cid to join him knew no bounds. Egged on by Rodrigo's old enemies, the Ordonez, he again pronounced a judgement of exile – this time backing it up by confiscating all El Cid's lands and goods. He even went so far as to imprison Rodrigo's wife Ximena, and his children; and though he soon released them he refused to listen to El Cid's demand to settle his innocence by right of combat. For the second time, and only two years after his triumphal return, Rodrigo was again in exile. This time he was virtually friendless, and his old comrade and employer, Motamid had died, leaving his son Mostain to rule over Saragossa. El

An eleventh-century manuscript's depiction of war between Christians and Moors, and its inevitable outcome — baptism or execution.

21

Cid's future seemed anything but happy, yet events were to take a dramatic turn in the months ahead.

The Struggle for Valencia

Exiled for the second time and without the support of many of the Castilian knights who had followed him before, Rodrigo once again displayed his qualities of a great commander. With a greatly reduced army, he marched into the kingdoms of Deria and Lerida. Capturing two strong castles, which he made his base, he secured a whole caveful of treasure belonging to the Lord of Lerida.

With this money, he was able to pay all his supporters, and with this added incentive he pressed the Moorish Caliphs so hard that they submitted to him, sueing for peace in the April of 1090. Rodrigo then advanced again on Valencia with extra forces supplied by his recent enemies of Deria.

Al-Kadir, the timid and vacillating ruler of Valencia, capitulated without delay, restoring the tribute he had been paying to El Cid before his second banishment. Rodrigo marched into Valencia in triumph, only to learn that his old adversary Berenguer of Barcelona — who had never forgiven the Cid for capturing him in an earlier campaign — had formed an alliance with the Moorish lord of Lerida and El Cid's own sometime ally Mostain of Saragossa. He also visited Alfonso and tried to enlist his support. Rather to the surprise of all, the Emperor refused. Even without him, the force against which Rodrigo now found himself ranged was vastly superior to his own. Leaving the safety of Valencia, he marched swiftly to a wooded valley near Tevar and fortified the three entrances with stout barriers.

There followed a swingeing series of letters between Rodrigo and Berenguer, in which each accused the other of treachery and cowardice. El Cid's final reply ended:

Thou twittest me with being a knave and a traitor, but then thou hast a lying tongue . . . Thou vauntest much of conquering me, but victory is in the hands of the Almighty, not in thine. Enough then of words, and let us fight it out like very knights. Come quickly and receive thy wonted reward!

(Pidal)

While this exchange was going on, Rodrigo had allowed certain of his men to desert to the other side, taking with them the story that El Cid was about to escape by night through one of the passes. This achieved the objective of making Berenguer split his force into three groups, each to watch one of the passes from the valley.

There then followed a confused series of night manoeuvres, which

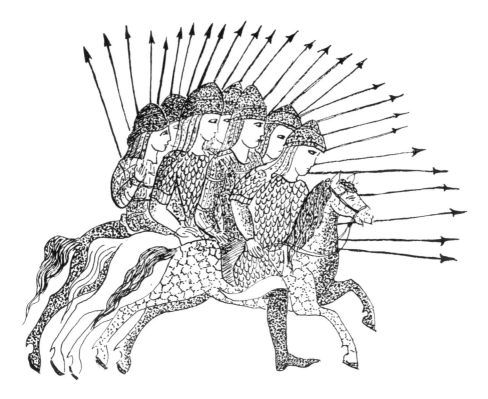

ended in confusion for both sides. Men from each force blundered to and fro in the darkness and El Cid himself was slightly wounded. However, his well-trained followers carried the assault without him, capturing Berenguer and 5000 of his men without any great losses of their own. The proud Count of Barcelona was thus forced to recognize the abilities of the man whose service he had once refused.

After this, most of the east and south-east of Moorish Spain offered tribute to El Cid, acknowledging him as their overlord and paying out 95,000 dinars a year for his protection.

By 1090 Rodrigo had succeeded in establishing a huge protectorate in the east which he found increasingly hard to maintain. Yusuf had returned briefly to Spanish soil, only to depart again, leaving behind a sizeable force of men. Consequently, there was a constant danger of those Moorish princes owing allegiance to El Cid calling upon him for aid, or simply reneging on their agreements and going over in force to the Almoravid leader.

This delicate balance had to be maintained. Rodrigo strove mightily not to offend his Moorish subjects, especially in Valencia which became his base of operations over the succeeding months. He ruled with justice and mercy, befriending the Moors rather than seeking to overpower them with his presence.

Such was the success of El Cid's enlightened rule that even Alfonso began to follow suit, ceasing his raids on the Andalusian Moors and

El Cid's charging cavalrymen, riding in a tightly disciplined formation, could strike at their enemy with tremendous force, wheeling and then retreating swiftly.

23

seeking treaties rather than warfare. Slowly, what was beginning to emerge – largely as a result of El Cid's efforts – was a Spanish kingdom where both Christian and Moor could live at peace.

So successful was the new pattern that when Yusuf made a third entry into Spain in 1090, he met with absolutely no support from the Caliphs; they either ignored him or actually placed obstacles in his path. The Almoravid chieftain's desire was to reconquer Toledo. He failed in this and retired, as Ramon Pidal puts it, 'completely baffled', leaving Alfonso and El Cid in a position of even greater strength.

The King now prepared to mount an attack on Granada and, thanks to the request of his queen in a personal letter to Rodrigo, El Cid joined him, raising the siege of Leira just as the city was about to capitulate rather than fail Alfonso.

But once again, El Cid's loyalty proved insufficient to satisfy the King. Although the two men rode together to Granada, Rodrigo made the mistake of pitching his tents closer than Alfonso's to the walls of the city. In this he was probably hoping to answer those who had claimed that fear was the cause of his failure to appear during the campaign at Valencia. Alfonso chose to see this as a further sign of Rodrigo's pride; once again the two men parted without reconciliation.

The brief moment of semi-unity in Spain was over almost before it had begun. Yusuf's forces returned in strength and began to win back many of the states so recently conquered by Alfonso and by El Cid in their separate campaigns. Within two years, all trace of Alfonso's Moorish protectorate in Granada and Andalusia had vanished. The Almoravids held the south firmly. Only Rodrigo now stood between them and prevented the whole of Moslem Spain from reverting to independent Moorish rule.

From Valencia, El Cid began to show his true strength, gradually extending his sway until he was virtual ruler of the great part of eastern Spain. At forty-five years of age he was at the height of his powers, determined to drive out the Almoravids and bring about a united Spain. To this end, he began to negotiate with other Christian princes. Unlike Alfonso, they chose to recognize his worth and to aid him in the war against the African Moors.

Knowing that the more treaties he himself signed, the greater would be the King's suspicion, Rodrigo did his utmost to bring about peace between Moslem lords and Christian princes.

Initially, Alfonso tried to frustrate his plans, but after El Cid had firmly put an end to the power of his old enemy Garcia Ordonez, the King gave way and finally revoked El Cid's exile.

Rodrigo now stood solidly as a unique power in the east. Valencia, over which he was only nominal ruler, became virtually a kingdom with El Cid as its Lord. His deeds had made his name synonymous with victory; the Almoravids feared and hated him; he had overcome all his

enemies and won his way back to the position of Alfonso's vassal – although, in fact, he overshadowed the King in such a way that Alfonso virtually faded from the scene in the next few years. It was Rodrigo's actions that now stood out in the notice of the people: it was El Cid's name they called in the streets.

In the middle of the year 1092, Rodrigo journeyed to Saragossa, where he received a friendly welcome from Mostain, and began to prepare his assault on the Almoravids in the south of the country. He was away from Valencia for a total of nine months and in that time two dramatic events took place. Yusuf sent a large force into Valencia and every fortress along the road to the city surrendered without a fight. When the Almoravid general sent a token force of twenty mounted warriors to the gates of the city, their arrival caused such consternation that it was believed that there were actually 500 or more. Panic spread through the city, followed by rebellion in the royal palace. The ageing king, Al-Kadir, was murdered and one of his viziers proclaimed the new overlord.

When news of this reached El Cid, he at once set out for his city but already in a matter of ten days, much of what he had achieved was undone. Granada, Seville, Malaga, Almeria, Murcia and Deria all fell to Yusuf's triumphant hoard. Rodrigo raised his standard at Juballa, a strong castle on the borders of Valencia, and from there began to raise an army to reconquer the city which had so recently been under his command. He sent a letter demanding its surrender, but its new ruler replied that the mighty Yusuf was near at hand and that if El Cid wished, he, the ruler of Valencia, would use his influence to gain El Cid a position under the true ruler of Spain!

Rodrigo now began a systematic war of attrition, biting deep into Valencian territory and reducing several of its castles to rubble. He also raided the villages around the city itself, carrying off cattle and prisoners. A poor response from Valencia was easily overcome and within the city there was much murmuring against the new ruler.

Within a month, Valencia was virtually an island in the middle of El Cid's forces; by July they were ready to sue for peace, which Rodrigo granted, on condition that all Almoravid soldiers left immediately.

With this achieved and with Rodrigo again in command of Valencia, the cards were dealt for the last hand between the Champion of Spain and the wily Moorish Emir. Yusuf had written demanding that El Cid leave Valencia at once. Rodrigo replied, in a letter which was sent to all the Moslem rulers, implying that Yusuf did not dare to cross the sea and face him.

In fact, it was to be another two years before the situation changed radically. In that time, there were frequent skirmishes between the Christians and Almoravids, and Valencia several times closed its gates to El Cid while he was engaged in campaigning in other parts of the country. Finally, on 15th June 1094, the city gave itself up totally to Rodrigo after a siege that had lasted nineteen months. This time, there was no question of nominal suzerainty: El Cid was virtually King of Valencia, though uncrowned. He sent for his wife and their three children, who took up residence with him in the old palace.

Now, Christian knights from all over Spain began to flock to his banner. Soon El Cid was able to count upon a force of some 8000 Christians and three times that number of Moslem warriors, both from Valencia itself and from Saragossa, Tortossa and Albarracin.

But Yusuf could no longer allow the continuance of El Cid's foothold in the east. He therefore despatched a force of some 150,000 horse and 3000 foot soldiers under the generalship of his nephew Mohammed, with orders to crush the power of the Campeador for ever.

Vengeance and Death

The battle of Cuarte took place near Valencia in December 1094. Here, the Christian forces defeated the Almoravids resoundingly, killing and driving off literally thousands of the Moors. El Cid himself fought like ten men and when he returned to the city he was bloody but victorious. He had used new tactics against the Moors, riding out suddenly at the head of a force of heavily armoured and mounted knights. They cut a swathe through the massed black-clad warriors, and then turning swiftly trampled back over their disorganized ranks. Legend has it that it was here that Yusuf met his death beneath the hooves of his enemies' steeds; here also that El Cid received a fatal wound. In reality, Yusuf was not even present and El Cid was to live for several more years.

The *Poema del Cid* describes his return to Valencia, where he was greeted by Ximena and their daughters:

See the bloody sword and sweating steed;
thus are Moors vanquished on the field.

The booty from the battle was tremendous. Rodrigo himself acquired 1000 horses, and he sent 200 of these to Alfonso along with the elaborate silken tent of the Almoravid leader, its carved posts decorated with gold.

Battle between two opposing groups of eleventh-century knights. Note the small round shields and long mail coats.

27

So complete was this victory that it ensured a kind of uneasy peace for nearly three years. Then, in 1097, Yusuf returned to Spain once more. In the fighting which ensued, Rodrigo's son Diego was slain, fighting alongside Alfonso, El Cid having remained in Valencia waiting for an attack which never came.

So great was Rodrigo's grief that he was almost paralysed for several weeks. Not only was the death of Diego the cause of personal sorrow, it also spelled the end of his family line.

Now aged fifty-four years, Rodrigo was still a splendid figure, possessed of as much energy and strength as in his youth – but he had campaigned almost unceasingly for nearly thirty years against the Moors and against Christian enemies. He had been wounded several times, twice seriously enough to have his life despaired of; he had twice suffered the rigours of exile. All this had taken its toll and there was no opportunity to rest or recover from either private loss or public defeat.

Gathering a new army, El Cid advanced on the Moorish forces, then holding the Castle of Murviedo in some strength. He laid siege to the fortress and gradually weakened it to the point of collapse. But the siege was to drag on into the summer of 1098 before the fortress finally capitulated and Rodrigo was able to enter in triumph and order Mass to be sung in one of the main squares.

With this, El Cid at once avenged the death of his son and once again showed that any attempt to reconquer Valencia was fruitless while he still lived. But the long-expected battle between the Campeador and the Emir was not to be. By now in his eighties, Yusuf would never again return to Spain – he too had been worn down by long years of struggle to remove the thorn of El Cid from his side. At best, he would now only send fresh generals against the Christian force; but even after El Cid's death, much of the heart had gone out of the Moorish invaders.

Rodrigo died suddenly at Valencia on Sunday, 10th July, 1099. He was fifty-five and still filled with plans for a united Spain. Ximena, who survived him by fifteen years, held Valencia for only a short time. It was only a matter of months before she was forced to withdraw even with the support of Alfonso (who now that the Cid was dead finally recognized the worth of his finest knight). Valencia returned to Moslem rule, along with the majority of the lands won back by Rodrigo's efforts.

Alfonso himself did not die until 1134 but, without the power of El Cid's support, he made no further inroads against the Moors.

But the idea of a united Spain did not completely die with El Cid. In time, the borders between Christian and Moslem grew more blurred, though there were many bloody wars still to be fought. During that time Spain became a cultural bridgehead between east and west. El Cid's remarkable achievements were recorded in poem and song, and grew with the telling until he became Spain's national hero. It is to the history of some of these works that one must turn for the last part of the story.

Poema del Cid and its Sources

Only eleven years after El Cid's death, a Moorish historian named Ibn Alcama wrote an account of the fall of Valencia, which he had witnessed, under the title *Eloquent Evidence of the Great Calamity*. He blamed the fall of the city on the impiety and general degeneracy of the people, who had

Monument to El Cid Campeador at Burgos, near which he was born.

been so foolish as to ally themselves with Christians in the first place. Not surprisingly, he spent a considerable amount of space vilifying the enemies of Islam.

As one would expect, this work, together with one by the Portuguese Moor Ibn Bassam, is virulently opposed to El Cid. Nevertheless, it is to these two writers that we owe almost all that we know of El Cid's life from those who were his contemporaries. They enable us to see how much of the *Poema* is romantic decoration (actually very little) and to fit the high points of the story into the larger context of medieval Spain.

The only near contemporary Christian account, the anonymous *Historia Roderici* (of about 1110) is only concerned with two aspects of El Cid's life – his heroism and his unfailing loyalty towards Alfonso. All episodes which do not illustrate these two Christian virtues are omitted, giving only a biased, pietistic portrait of an idealized figure.

Next comes a fragmentary Latin poem known as the *Carmen*, which deals with the struggle between El Cid and the counts of Barcelona. Then, some forty years after Rodrigo's death, comes the *Poema del Cid*, one of the truly great works of medieval literature and the work from which the exploits of El Cid are generally known. It exists as a single manuscript, probably dating from 1245. It shows strong stylistic similarities to other medieval romances, in particular the *Chansons de Geste* of Charlemagne and the *Song of Roland*.

Although the emphasis of the *Poema* is on the heroic qualities of El Cid, we have a more fully rounded portrait of his life, marriage, family and exile. Also included are episodes which show Rodrigo in a less than heroic light. He is described as playing tricks on Jewish moneylenders in order to finance his soldiery, and generally behaving in a manner very far from what one might expect from the deeds of similar heroes such as Roland, Ogier or Lancelot.

Not that the anonymous author of the *Poema* ever criticizes his hero – the whole work shines with an almost feverish air of hero-worship. Rodrigo is always 'my Cid', as though the writer felt a degree of affection for his hero beyond that of author and subject. Indeed, the possibility that he may actually have known Rodrigo cannot be ruled out, and offers a tantalizing possibility that we may be reading a first-hand account.

After the *Poema* there were to be no more serious attempts to re-tell the life of El Cid with any fidelity to actual events. King Alfonso X 'the Wise', commissioned a vast chronicle of Spanish history, the *Primeva Cronica General de Espana* (c. 1289). It was written not in Latin, but in the Romance language. This drew not only on *bona fide* sources, but upon poetry, ballads and pseudo-history.

Once again, as with heroes such as Arthur, Charlemagne and Macbeth, an original core of genuine history gathered about it a coating of myth and legend which distorted the truth and added extensively to the apocryphal side of Rodrigo's life.

This set the pattern for all later accounts of El Cid up to the seventeenth century, when medieval sources were frequently questioned as to their ultimate accuracy.

From this point onwards, attitudes to El Cid were divided. They included, on the one hand, the eulogistic writings of the nineteenth century Swiss historian Johann Muller, who wrote that:

All that godliness, honour and love could make of a knight was combined in Don Rodrigo . . . This remarkable man is one of the few who . . . have been, in their own lifetime, their country's pride

(trans: Sunderland.)

But, on the other hand, they ranged to the equally fervent, though dissatisfied Masden, the Jesuit who described the earlier works as catalogues of the 'perfidy, perjury and brazen deeds of Rodrigo Diaz.' (Sunderland, after Pidal.)

After this, the figure of El Cid entered a dark period in which historian after historian, following a 1849 work of the Dutch orientalist R. Dozy, contrived to portray Rodrigo as a cruel, treacherous and often barbarian character.

Assyrian soldiers at the seige of Jerusalem in 1099. Their armour and weapons reflect perfectly the influence of both Christian and Moorish arms. Warriors who fought with El Cid would have employed such an amalgam of both kinds of weaponry.

31

Not until the enlightened work of Ramon Menendez Pidal in the first half of the twentieth century, was the figure of El Cid re-established in something like a clear light. Any writer dealing with Rodrigo must turn to Pidal, and this present work could certainly not have been accomplished without his scrupulous and immensely detailed account of the life and period of El Cid.

The memory of the heroism and sterling qualities of Rodrigo del Bivar have thus been enshrined for all time; his statue stands today in the main square of Burgos, staring out forever across the lands he fought so long to transform.

He was a hero of the old style, whose life and deeds left their mark on the tide of human history and became the inspiration of a whole nation.

The Life and Deeds of El Cid Campeador

The following extracts are from the earliest translation of the story of El Cid. Robert Southey (1774–1843) who was later to become poet laureate, discovered the medieval *Chronica del Cid* during his childhood in Spain, and later made a translation which became something of a best-seller in the nineteenth century. The story it tells is close to the historical details already described, but there is an overlay of romanticism which brings the dry facts to life. This selection also includes several episodes not dealt with in the first half of this book, but which are an integral part of El Cid's legend. They are arranged to make a more or less connected narrative, and, taken within the larger historical framework already described, form a more detailed story of El Cid.

The headings of the sections and the linking passages were created especially for inclusion in this selection, but the spellings and names are those used in the original extracts.

The Rise of Rodrigo del Bivar

King Don Ferdinand succeeded to the states of Castille after the death of his father King Don Sancho el Mayor, in the era 1072, which was the year of the Incarnation 1034, and from the coming of the Patriarch Tubal to settle in Spain 3197, and from the general deluge 3339, and from the creation of the world 4995, according to the computation of the Hebrews, and from the beginning of the false sect of the Moors 413. And in the year 1037 Ferdinand slew Bermudo the King of Leon in battle, who was his wife's brother, and conquered his kingdom, and succeeded to it in right of his wife Doña Sancha. So he was the first person who united the states of Castille and Leon, and the first who was called King of

Having defeated a large Christian force, the Moorish Emir Yusuf orders the heads of his foes cut off and piled in mounds. From the top of one of these, a muezzin calls the faithful to prayer.

Castille; for till this time the lords of that country had been called Counts. He was a good king, and one who judged justly and feared God, and was bold in all his doings. Before he reigned he had, by Doña Sancha his wife the Infanta Doña Urraca, his eldest daughter, who was a right excellent lady, and after her he had the Infante Don Sancho, his eldest son and heir; and then the Infanta Doña Elvira, whom after the death of the King her father, her brother King Don Alfonso married to the Count Don Garcia de Cabra. And after he became King he had the Infante Don Alfonso, and the Infante Don Garcia, who was the youngest of all. And he put his sons to read, that they might be of the better understanding, and he made them take arms, and be shown how to demean themselves in battle, and to be huntsmen. And he ordered that his daughters should be brought up in the studies beseeming dames.

In those days arose Rodrigo of Bivar, who was a youth strong in arms and of good customs; and the people rejoiced in him, for he bestirred himself to protect the land from the Moors.

At this time it came to pass that there was strife between Count Don Gomez the Lord of Gormaz, and Diego Laynez the father of Rodrigo; and the Count insulted Diego and gave him a blow. Now Diego was a man in years, and his strength had passed from him, so that he could not take vengeance, and he retired to his home to dwell there in solitude and lament over his dishonour. And he took no pleasure in his food, neither could he sleep by night, nor would he lift up his eyes from the ground, nor stir out of his house, nor commune with his friends, but turned from them in silence as if the breath of his shame would taint them. Rodrigo was yet but a youth, and the Count was a mighty man in arms, one who gave his voice first in the Cortes, and was held to be the best in the war, and so powerful that he had a thousand friends among the mountains. Howbeit all these things appeared as nothing to Rodrigo when he thought of the wrong done to his father, the first which had ever been offered to the blood of Layn Calvo. He asked nothing but justice of Heaven, and of man he asked only a fair field; and his father seeing of how good heart he was, gave him his sword and his blessing. The sword had been the sword of Mudarra in former times, and when Rodrigo held its cross in his hand, he thought within himself that his arm was not weaker than Mudarra's. And he went out and defied the Count and slew him, and smote off his head and carried it home to his father. The old man was sitting at table, the food lying before him untasted, when Rodrigo returned, and pointing to the head which hung from the horse's collar, dropping blood, he bade him look up, for there was the herb which should restore to him his appetite. The tongue, quoth he, which insulted you is no longer a tongue, and the hand which wronged you is no longer a hand. And the old man arose and embraced his son and placed him above him at the table, saying, that he who had brought home that head should be the head of the house of Layn Calvo.

In the Great Hall of Burgos, El Cid forces the treacherous King Alfonso to swear an oath on sacred relics that he had no part in his own brother's death. Alfonso is thus humbled and perjured before his nobles.

After this Diego being full of years fell asleep and was gathered to his fathers. And the Moors entered Castille, in great power, for there came with them five Kings, and they past above Burgos, and crost the mountains of Oca, and plundered Carrion, and Vilforado, and Saint Domingo de la Calzada, and Logroño, and Najara, and all that land; and they carried away many captives both male and female, and brood mares, and flocks of all kinds. But as they were returning with all speed, Rodrigo of Bivar raised the country, and came up with them in the mountains of Oca, and fell upon them and discomfited them, and won back all their booty, and took all the five Kings prisoners. Then he went back to his mother, taking the Kings with him, and there he divided the whole spoil with the hidalgos and his other companions, both the Moorish captives and all the spoil of whatever kind, so that they departed right joyfully, being well pleased with what he had done. And he gave thanks to God for the grace which had been vouchsafed to him, and said to his mother, that he did not think it good to keep the Kings in captivity, but to let them go freely; and he set them at liberty and bade them depart. So they returned each to his own country, blessing him for their deliverance, and magnifying his great bounty; and forthwith they sent him tribute and acknowledged themselves to be his vassals.

King Don Ferdinand was going through Leon, putting the Kingdom in order, when tidings reached him of the good speed which Rodrigo had had against the Moors. And at the same time there came before him Ximena Gomez, the daughter of the Count, who fell on her knees before him and said, Sir, I am the daughter of Count Don Gomez of Gormaz, and Rodrigo of Bivar has slain the Count my father, and of three daughters whom he has left I am the youngest. And, Sir, I come to crave of you a boon, that you will give me Rodrigo of Bivar to be my husband, with whom I shall hold myself well married, and greatly honoured; for certain I am that his possessions will one day be greater than those of any man in your dominions. Certes, Sir, it behoves you to do this, because it is for God's service, and because I may pardon Rodrigo with a good will. The King held it good to accomplish her desire; and forthwith ordered letters to be drawn up to Rodrigo of Bivar, wherein he enjoined and commanded him that he should come incontinently to Valencia, for he had much to communicate to him, upon an affair which was greatly to God's service, and his own welfare and great honour.

When Rodrigo saw the letters of his Lord the King, he greatly rejoiced in them, and said to the messengers that he would fulfil the King's pleasure, and go incontinently to his command. And he dight himself full gallantly and well, and took with him many knights, both his own and of his kindred and of his friends, and he took also many new arms, and came to Valencia to the King with two hundred of his peers in arms, in festival guise; and the King went out to meet him, and received him right well, and did him honour; and at this were all the Counts

34

displeased. And when the King thought it a fit season, he spake to him and said, that Doña Ximena Gomez, the daughter of the Count whom he had slain, had come to ask him for her husband, and would forgive him her father's death; wherefore he besought him to think it good to take her to be his wife, in which case he would show him great favour. When Rodrigo heard this it pleased him well, and he said to the King that he would do his bidding in this, and in all other things which he might command; and the King thanked him much. And he sent for the Bishop of Valencia, and took their vows and made them plight themselves each to the other according as the law directs. And when they were espoused the King did them great honour, and gave them many noble gifts, and added to Rodrigo's lands more than he had till then possessed: and he loved him greatly in his heart, because he saw that he was obedient to his commands, and for all that he had heard him say.

So Rodrigo departed from the King, and took his spouse with him to the house of his mother, and gave her to his mother's keeping. And forthwith he made a vow in her hands that he would never accompany with her, neither in the desert nor in the inhabited place, till he had won five battles in the field. And he besought his mother that she would love her even as she loved him himself, and that she would do good to her and show her great honour, for which he should ever serve her with the better good will. And his mother promised him so to do; and then he departed from them and went out against the frontier of the Moors.

The Cathedral of San Isidoro, Leon. Here the Spanish kings were buried.

How Rodrigo Met with a Leper

Rodrigo set out upon the road, and took with him twenty knights. And as he went he did great good, and gave alms, feeding the poor and needy. And upon the way they found a leper, struggling in a quagmire, who cried out to them with a loud voice to help him for the love of God; and when Rodrigo heard this, he alighted from his beast and helped him, and placed him upon the beast before him, and carried him with him in this manner to the inn where he took up his lodging that night. At this were his knights little pleased. And when supper was ready he bade his knights take their seats, and he took the leper by the hand, and seated him next himself, and ate with him out of the same dish. The knights were greatly offended at this foul sight, insomuch that they rose up and left the chamber. But Rodrigo ordered a bed to be made ready for himself and for the leper, and they twain slept together. When it was midnight and Rodrigo was fast asleep, the leper breathed against him between his shoulders, and that breath was so strong that it passed through him, even through his breast; and he awoke, being astounded, and felt for the leper by him, and found him not; and he began to call him, but there was no reply. Then he arose in fear, and called for light, and it was brought him; and he looked for the leper and could see nothing; so he returned into the bed, leaving the light burning. And he began to think within himself what had happened, and of that breath which had passed through him, and how the leper was not there. After a while, as he was thus musing, there appeared before him one in white garments, who said unto him, Sleepest thou or wakest thou, Rodrigo? and he answered and said, I do not sleep: but who art thou that bringest with thee such brightness and so sweet an odour? Then said he, I am Saint Lazarus, and know that I was the leper to whom thou didst so much good and so great honour for the love of God; and because thou didst this for his sake hath God now granted thee a great gift; for whensoever that breath which thou hast felt shall come upon thee whatever thing thou desires to do, and shalt then begin, that shalt thou accomplish to thy heart's desire, whether it be in battle or aught else, so thy honour shall go on increasing from day to day; and thou shalt be feared both by Moors and Christians, and thy enemies shall never prevail against thee, and thou shalt die an honourable death in thine own house, and in thy renown, for God hath blessed thee; – therefore go thou on, and evermore persevere in doing good; and with that he disappeared.

How El Cid was Exiled

[Now] . . . King Don Alfonso assembled together all his power and went against the Moors. And the Cid should have gone with him, but he fell sick and perforce therefore abode at home. And while the King was going through Andalusia, having the land at his mercy, a great power of the Moors assembled together on the other side, and entered the land,

and besieged the castle of Gormaz, and did much evil. At this time the Cid was gathering strength; and when he heard that the Moors were in the country, laying waste before them, he gathered together what force he could, and went after them; and the Moors, when they heard this, dared not abide his coming, but began to fly. And the Cid followed them to Atienza, and to Ciguenza, and Fita, and Guadalajara, and through the whole land of St. Esteban, as far as Toledo, slaying and burning, and plundering and destroying, and laying hands on all whom he found, so that he brought back seven thousand prisoners, men and women; and he and all his people returned rich and with great honour. But when the King of Toledo heard of the hurt which he had received at the hands of the Cid, he sent to King Don Alfonso to complain thereof, and the King was greatly troubled. And then the Ricos-omes who wished ill to the Cid, had the way open to do him evil with the King, and they said to the King, Sir Ruydiez hath broken your faith, and the oath and promise which you made to the King of Toledo: and he hath done this for no other reason but that the Moors of Toledo may fall upon us here, and slay both you and us. And the King believed what they said, and was wroth against the Cid, having no love towards him because of the oath which he had pressed upon him at Burgos concerning the death of King Don Sancho his brother. And he went with all speed to Burgos, and sent from thence to bid the Cid come unto him.

Now my Cid knew the evil disposition of the King towards him, and when he received his bidding, he made answer that he would meet him between Burgos and Bivar. And the King went out from Burgos and came nigh unto Bivar; and the Cid came up to him and would have kissed his hand, but the King withheld it, and said angrily unto him, Ruydiez, quit my land. Then the Cid clapt spurs to the mule upon which he rode, and vaulted into a piece of ground which was his own inheritance, and answered, Sir, I am not in your land, but in my own. And the King replied full wrathfully, Go out of my kingdoms without any delay. And the Cid made answer, Give me then thirty days time, as is the right of the hidalgos; and the King said he would come and look for him. The Counts were well pleased at this; but all the people of the land were sorrowful. And then the King and the Cid parted. And the Cid sent for all his friends and his kinsmen and vassals, and told them how King Don Alfonso had banished him from the land, and asked of them who would follow him into banishment, and who would remain at home. Then Alvar Fañez, who was his cousin-german, came forward and said, Cid, we will all go with you, through desert and through peopled country, and never fail you. In your service will we spend our mules and horses, our wealth and our garments, and ever while we live be unto you loyal friends and vassals. And they all confirmed what Alvar Fañez had said; and the Cid thanked them for their love, and said that there might come a time in which he should guerdon them.

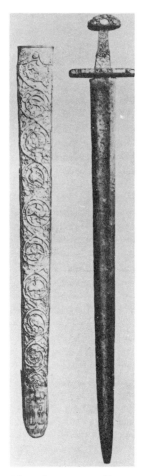

Eleventh century German sword and sheath of the type carried by Rodrigo's followers.

And as he was about to depart he looked back upon his own home, and when he saw his hall deserted, the household chests unfastened, the doors open, no cloaks hanging up, no seats in the porch, no hawks upon the perches, the tears came into his eyes, and he said, My enemies have done this . . . God be praised for all things. And he turned toward the East and knelt and said, Holy Mary Mother, and all Saints, pray to God for me, that he may give me strength to destroy all the Pagans, and to win enough from them to requite my friends therewith, and all those who follow and help me. Then he called for Alvar Fañez and said unto him, Cousin, the poor have no part in the wrong which the King hath done us; see now that no wrong be done unto them along our road: and he called for his horse. And then an old woman who was standing at her door said, Go in a lucky minute, and make spoil of whatever you wish. And with this proverb he rode on, saying, Friends, by God's good pleasure we shall return to Castille with great honour and great gain. And as they went out from Bivar they had a crow on their right hand, and when they came to Burgos they had a crow on the left.

How the Moors of Africa First Came to Spain
Now came true tidings to Valencia that the host of the Almoravides were coming, and that they were now at Lorca, and the son in law of the Miramamolin at their head, for he himself could not come, by reason that he ailed. They of Valencia took courage at these tidings, and waxed insolent, and began to devise how they should take vengeance upon Abeniaf, and upon all those who had oppressed them. And Abeniaf was in great trouble at this which was said openly concerning him, and he sent privily to the Cid, telling him to come as soon as might be. The Cid was then before Albarrazin, doing all the evil that he could, and he brake up his camp and came with his host to Juballa; and Abeniaf and the Alcaydes of Xativa and Carchayra came unto him, and they renewed their covenant to stand by each other, and be of one voice. And they took counsel and made a letter for the leader of the army of the Almoravides, wherein they told him that the Cid had made a treaty with the King of Aragon, whereby the King bound himself to help him against them; and they bade him beware how he came towards Valencia, unless he chose to do battle with eight thousand Christian horsemen, covered with iron, and the best warriors in the world. This did they thinking that he would be dismayed and turn back: but the Moor did not cease to advance, notwithstanding this letter.

How El Cid Entered Valencia
On the following day after the Christians had taken possession of the town, the Cid entered it with a great company, and he ascended the highest tower of the wall, and beheld all the city; and the Moors came unto him, and kissed his hand, saying he was welcome. And the Cid did

38

great honour unto them. And then he gave order that all the windows of the towers which looked in upon the town should be closed up, that the Christians might not see what the Moors did in their houses; and the Moors thanked him for this greatly. And he commanded and requested the Christians that they should show great honour to the Moors, and respect them, and greet them when they met: and the Moors thanked the Cid greatly for the honour which the Christians did them, saying that they had never seen so good a man, nor one so honourable, nor one who had his people under such obedience.

And when they were all assembled, he went out unto them, to a place which was made ready with carpets and with mats, and he made them take their seats before him full honourably, and began to speak unto them, saying, I am a man who have never possessed a kingdom, neither I nor any man of my lineage. But the day when I first beheld this city I was well pleased therewith, and coveted it that I might be its Lord; and I besought the Lord our God that he would give it me. See now what his power is, for the day when I sate down before Juballa I had no more than four loaves of bread, and now by God's mercy I have won Valencia. And if I administer right and justice here God will let me enjoy it, but if I do evil, and demean myself proudly and wrongfully, I know that he will take it away. Now then let every one go to his own lands, and possess them even as he was wont to have and to hold them. He who shall find his field, or his vineyard, or his garden, desert, let him incontinently enter thereon; and he who shall find his husbanded, let him pay him that hath cultivated it the cost of his labour, and of the seed which he hath sown therein, and remain with his heritage, according to the law of the Moors. Moreover I have given order that they who collect my dues take from you no more than the tenth, because so it is appointed by the custom of the Moors, and it is what ye have been wont to pay. And I have resolved in my heart to hear your complaints two days in the week, on the Monday and the Thursday; but if causes should arise which require haste, come to me when ye will and I will give judgment, for I do not retire with women to sing and to drink, as your Lords have done, so that ye could obtain no justice, but will myself see to these things, and watch over ye as friend over his friend, and kinsman over his kinsman. And I will be Cadi and Guanzil, and when dispute happens among ye I will decide it. When he had said these things they all replied that they prayed God to preserve him through long and happy years, and four of the most honourable among them rose and kissed his hands, and the Cid bade them take their seats again.

How the Moors Attacked Valencia

The winter is past, and March is coming in. Three months Doña Ximena had been in Valencia, when tidings came to the Cid from beyond sea, that King Yucef, the son of the Miramamolin, who dwelt in Morocco,

Spanish soldier from the door of a Spanish cathedral. His shield and spear show graphically the arms carried by El Cid's armies.

39

was coming to lay siege unto Valencia with fifty thousand men. When the Cid heard this he gave command to store all his Castles, and had them well repaired. And he had the walls of the city prepared, and stored it well with food and with all things needful for war, and gathered together a great power of Christians and of the Moors of his seignory. Hardly had he done this before he heard that Yucef was near at hand, and coming as fast as he could come. Then the Cid assembled together the Christians in the Alcazar, and when they were assembled, he rose upon his feet and said, Friends and kinsmen and vassals, praised be God and holy Mary Mother, all the good which I have in the world I have here in Valencia; with hard labour I won the city, and hold it for my heritage, and for nothing less than death will I leave it. My daughters and my wife shall see me fight, . . . they shall see with their own eyes our manner of living in this land, and how we get our bread. We will go out against the Moors and give them battle, and God who hath thus far shown favour unto us will still continue to be our helper. When they heard this they cried out with one accord that they would do his bidding, and go out with him and fight under his banner, for certain they were that by his good fortune the Moors would be overthrown.

On the morrow the Cid took Doña Ximena by the hand, and her daughters with her, and made them go up upon the highest tower of the Alcazar, and they looked toward the sea and saw the great power of the Moors, how they came on and drew nigh, and began to pitch their tents round about Valencia, beating their tambours and with great uproar. And Ximena's heart failed her, and she asked the Cid if peradventure God would deliver him from these enemies. Fear not, honoured woman, said he; you are but lately arrived, and they come to bring you a present, which shall help marry your daughters. Fear not, for you shall see me fight by the help of God and holy Mary Mother; my heart kindles because you are here! The more Moors the more gain! The tambours sounded now with a great alarum, and the sun was shining . . . Cheer up, said my Cid; . . . this is a glorious day. But Ximena was seized with such fear as if her heart would have broken; she and her daughters had never been in such fear since the day that they were born. Then the good Cid Campeador stroked his beard and said, Fear not, all this is for your good. Before fifteen days are over, if it please God, those tambours shall be laid before you, and shall be sounded for your pleasure, and then they shall be given to the Bishop Don Hieronymo, that he may hang them up in the Church of St. Mary, Mother of God. This vow the Cid Campeador made. Now the Moors began to enter the gardens which were round about the town, and the watchman saw them and struck the bell. My Cid looked back and saw Alvar Salvadores beside him, and he said, go now, take two hundred horse, and sally upon yonder Moors who are entering the gardens; let Doña Ximena and her daughters see the good will you have to serve them. Down went Alvar Salvadores in great haste, and ordered a bell to be rung which was a signal for two hundred knights to make ready; for the history saith, that the Cid, by reason that he was alway in war, had appointed such signals for his people, that they knew when one hundred were called for, and when two, and so forth. Presently they were ready at the place of meeting, and the gate was opened which was nearest the gardens where the Moors had entered, without order; and they fell fiercely upon them, smiting and slaying. Great was the pleasure of the Cid at seeing how well they behaved themselves. And Doña Ximena and her daughters stood trembling, like women who had never seen such things before: and when the Cid saw it he made them seat themselves, so as no longer to behold it. Great liking had the Bishop Don Hieronymo to see how bravely they fought. Alvar Salvadores and his companions bestirred themselves so well that they drove the enemy to their tents, making great mortality among them, and then they turned back, whereat my Cid was well pleased; but Alvar Salvadores went on, hacking and hewing all before him, for he thought the ladies were looking on, and he pressed forward so far, that being without succour he was taken. The others returned to the city, falling back in brave order till they were out of reach of the enemy: and they had done no little in that exploit, for they slew above two hundred and fifty Moors. When my Cid saw that they who eat his bread were returned, he went down from the tower, and received them right well, and praised them for what they had done like good knights: howbeit he was full sorrowful for Alvar Salvadores that he should be in the hands of the Moors, but he trusted in God that he should deliver him on the morrow.

And the Cid assembled his chief captains and knights and people, and said unto them, Kinsmen and friends and vassals, hear me: to-day has been a good day, and to-morrow shall be a better day.

Four thousand, lacking thirty, were they who went out with my Cid, with a good will, to attack fifty thousand. They went through all the narrow places, and bad passes, and leaving the ambush on the left, struck to the right hand, so as to get the Moors between them and the town. And the Cid put his battles in good array, and bade Pero Bermudez bear his banner. When the Moors saw this they were greatly amazed; and they harnessed themselves in great haste, and came out of their tents. Then the Cid bade his banner move on, and the Bishop Don Hieronymo pricked forward with his company, and laid on with such guise, that the hosts were soon mingled together. Then might you have seen many a horse running about the field with the saddle under his belly, and many a horseman in evil plight upon the ground. Great was the smiting and slaying in short time; but by reason that the Moors were so great a number, they bore hard upon the Christians, and were in the hour of overcoming them. And the Cid began to encourage them with a loud voice, shouting God and Santiago! And Alvar Fañez at this time issued out from ambush, and fell upon them, on the side which was nearest the

Eleventh-century Norman knight with chain mail coat, kite-shaped shield, sword and long lance which could be used from horseback. With small variations, this is typical of the kind of armour worn by El Cid and his warriors.

41

sea; and the Moors thought that a great power had arrived to the Cid's succour, and they were dismayed, and began to fly. And the Cid and his people pursued, punishing them in a bad way. If we should wish to tell you how every one behaved himself in this battle, it is a thing which could not be done, for all did so well that no man can relate their feats. And the Cid Ruydiez did so well, and made such mortality among the Moors, that the blood ran from his wrist to his elbow! great pleasure had he in his horse Bavieca that day, to find himself so well mounted. And in the pursuit he came up to King Yucef, and smote him three times: but the King escaped from under the sword, for the horse of the Cid passed on in his course, and when he turned, the King being on a fleet horse, was far off, so that he might not be overtaken; and he got into a Castle called Guyera, for so far did the Christians pursue them, smiting and slaying, and giving them no respite, so that hardly fifteen thousand escaped of fifty that they were. And they who were in the ships, fled to Denia.

Then the Cid and his people returned to the field and began to plunder the tents. And the spoil was so great that there was no end to the riches, in gold and in silver, and in horses and arms, so that men knew not what to leave and what to take. And they found one tent which had been King Yucef's; never man saw so noble a thing as that tent was; and there were great riches therein, and there also did they find Alvar Salvadores, who had been made prisoner the yesterday, as ye have heard. Greatly did the Cid rejoice when he saw him alive and sound, and he ordered his chains to be taken off; and then he left Alvar Fañez to look to the spoil, and went into Valencia with a hundred knights. His wrinkled brow was seen, for he had taken off his helmet, and in this manner he entered, upon Bavieca, sword in hand. Great joy had Doña Ximena and her daughters, who were awaiting him, when they saw him come riding in; and he stopt when he came to them, and said, Great honour have I won for you, while you kept Valencia this day! God and the Saints have sent us goodly gain, upon your coming. Look, with a bloody sword, and a horse all sweat, this is the way that we conquer the Moors! Pray God that I may live yet awhile for your sakes, and you shall enter into great honour, and they shall kiss your hands. Then my Cid alighted when he had said this, and the ladies knelt down before him, and kissed his hand, and wished him long life. Then they entered the Palace with him, and took their seats upon the precious benches. Wife Doña Ximena, said he, these damsels who have served you so well, I will give in marriage to these my vassals, and to every one of them two hundred marks of silver, that it may be known in Castille what they have got by their services. Your daughters' marriage will come in time. And they all rose and kissed his hand; great was the joy in the Palace, it was done according as the Cid had said.

The Death of El Cid
The Cid sickened of the malady of which he died. And the day before his

weakness waxed great, he ordered the gates of the town to be shut, and went to the Church of St. Peter; and there the Bishop Don Hieronymo being present, and all the clergy who were in Valencia, and the knights and honourable men and honourable dames, as many as the Church could hold, the Cid Ruydiez stood up, and made a full noble preaching, showing that no man whatsoever, however honourable or fortunate they may be in this world, can escape death; to which, said he, I am now full near; and since ye know that this body of mine hath never yet been conquered, nor put to shame, I beseech ye let not this befall it at the end, for the good fortune of man is only accomplished at his end. How this is to be done, and what ye all have to do, I will leave in the hands of the Bishop Don Hieronymo, and Alvar Fañez, and Pero Bermudez. And when he had said this he placed himself at the feet of the Bishop, and there before all the people made a general confession of all his sins, and all the faults which he had committed against our Lord Jesus Christ. And the Bishop appointed him his penance, and assoyled him of his sins. Then he arose and took leave of the people, weeping plenteously, and returned to the Alcazar, and betook himself to his bed, and never rose from it again; and every day he waxed weaker and weaker, till seven days only remained of the time appointed. Then he called for the caskets of gold in which was the balsam and the myrrh which the Soldan of Persia had sent him; and when these were put before him he bade them bring him the golden cup, of which he was wont to drink; and he took of that balsam and of that myrrh as much as a little spoon-full, and mingled it in the cup with rose-water and drank of it; and for the seven days which he lived he neither ate nor drank aught else than a little of that myrrh and balsam mingled with water. And every day after he did this, his body and his countenance appeared fairer and fresher than before, and his voice clearer, though he waxed weaker and weaker daily, so that he could not move in his bed.

On the twenty-ninth day, being the day before he departed, he called for Doña Ximena, and for the Bishop Don Hieronymo, and Don Alvar Fañez Minaya, and Pero Bermudez, and his trusty Gil Diaz; and when they were all five before him, he began to direct them what they should do after his death; and he said to them, Ye know that King Bucar will presently be here to besiege this city, with seven and and thirty Kings whom he bringeth with him, and with a mighty power of Moors. Now therefore the first thing which ye do after I have departed, wash my body with rose-water many times and well, as blessed be the name of God it is washed within and made pure of all uncleanness to receive his holy body to-morrow, which will be my last day. And when it has been well washed and made clean, ye shall dry it well, and anoint it with this myrrh and balsam, from these golden caskets, from head to foot, so that every part shall be anointed, till none be left. And you my Sister Doña Ximena, and your women, see that ye utter no cries, neither make any lamenta-

Eleventh-century Spanish soldier in mail shirt and coif, with conical helmet and long shield. The lance would have been used both to stab and as a weapon from throwing or as a lance on horseback.

43

tion for me, that the Moors may not know of my death. And when the day shall come in which King Bucar arrives, order all the people of Valencia to go upon the walls, and sound your trumpets and tambours, and make the greatest rejoicing that ye can. And when ye would set out for Castille, let all the people know in secret, that they make themselves ready, and take with them all that they have, so that none of the Moors in the suburb may know thereof; for certes ye cannot keep the city, neither abide therein after my death. And see ye that sumpter beasts be laden with all that there is in Valencia, so that nothing which can profit may be left. And this I leave especially to your charge, Gil Diaz. Then saddle ye my horse Bavieca, and arm him well; and ye shall apparel my body full seemlily, and place me upon the horse, and fasten and tie me thereon so that it cannot fall: and fasten my sword Tizona in my hand. And let the Bishop Don Hieronymo go on one side of me, and my trusty Gil Diaz on the other, and he shall lead my horse. You, Pero Bermudez, shall bear my banner, as you were wont to bear it; and you, Alvar Fañez, my cousin, gather your company together, and put the host in order as you are wont to do. And go ye forth and fight with King Bucar: for be ye certain and doubt not that ye shall win this battle; God hath granted me this. And when ye have won the fight, and the Moors are discomfited, ye may spoil the field at pleasure. Ye will find great riches. What ye are afterwards to do I will tell ye to-morrow, when I make my testament.

Three days after the Cid had departed King Bucar came into the port of Valencia, and landed with all his power, which was so great that there is not a man in the world who could give account of the Moors whom he brought. And there came with him thirty and six Kings, and one Moorish Queen, who was a negress, and she brought with her two hundred horsewomen, all negresses like herself, all having their hair shorn save a tuft on the top, and this was in token that they came as if upon a pilgrimage, and to obtain the remission of their sins; and they were all armed in coats of mail and with Turkish bows. King Bucar ordered his tents to be pitched round about Valencia, and Abenalfarax who wrote this history in Arabic, saith, that there were full fifteen thousand tents; and he bade that Moorish negress with her archers to take their station near the city. And on the morrow they began to attack the city, and they fought against it three days strenuously; and the Moors received great loss, for they came blindly up to the walls and were slain there. And the Christians defended themselves right well, and every time that they went upon the walls, they sounded trumpets and tambours; and made great rejoicings, as the Cid had commanded. This continued for eight days or nine, till the companions of the Cid had made ready every thing for their departure, as he had commanded. And King Bucar and his people thought that the Cid dared not come out against them, and they were the more encouraged, and began to think of making bastilles and engines wherewith to combat the city, for certes they weened that the Cid Ruydiez dared not come out against them, seeing that he tarried so long.

All this while the company of the Cid were preparing all things to go into Castille, as he had commanded before his death; and his trusty Gil Diaz did nothing else but labour at this. And the body of the Cid was prepared after this manner: first it was embalmed and anointed as the history hath already recounted, and the virtue of the balsam and myrrh was such that the flesh remained firm and fair, having its natural colour, and his countenance as it was wont to be, and the eyes open, and his long beard in order, so that there was not a man who would have thought him dead if he had seen him and not known it. And on the second day after he had departed, Gil Diaz placed the body upon a right noble saddle, and this saddle with the body upon it he put upon a frame; and he dressed the body in a *gambax* of fine sendal, next the skin. And he took two boards and fitted them to the body, one to the breast and the other to the shoulders; these were so hollowed out and fitted that they met at the sides and under the arms, and the hind one came up to the pole, and the other up to the beard; and these boards were fastened into the saddle, so that the body could not move. All this was done by the morning of the twelfth day; and all that day the people of the Cid were busied in making ready their arms, and in loading beasts with all that they had, so that they left nothing of any price in the whole city of Valencia, save only the empty houses. When it was midnight they took the body of the Cid, fastened to the saddle as it was, and placed it upon his horse Bavieca, and fastened the saddle well: and the body sate so upright and well that it seemed as if he was alive. And it had on painted hose of black and white, so cunningly painted that no man who saw them would have thought but that they were grieves and cuishes, unless he had laid his hand upon them; and they put on it a surcoat of green sendal, having his arms blazoned thereon, and a helmet of parchment, which was cunningly painted that every one might have believed it to be iron; and his shield was hung round his neck, and they placed the sword Tizona in his hand, and they raised his arm, and fastened it up so subtilly that it was a marvel to see how upright he held the sword. And the Bishop Don Hieronymo went on one side of him, and the trusty Gil Diaz on the other, and he led the horse Bavieca, as the Cid had commanded him. And when all this had been made ready, they went out from Valencia at midnight, through the gate of Roseros, which is towards Castille. Pero Bermudez went first with the banner of the Cid, and with him five hundred knights who guarded it, all well appointed. And after these came all the baggage. Then came the body of the Cid with an hundred knights, all chosen men, and behind them Doña Ximena with all her company, and six hundred knights in the rear. All these went out so silently, and with such a measured pace, that it seemed as if there were only a score. And by the time that they had all gone out it was broad day.

Twelfth-century sword, much like the weapons carried by Rodrigo and his men.

45

Bronze dagger of Moorish design, carved with magical symbols to protect its user from harm and to inflict the maximum damage on those it struck.

Now Alvar Fañez Minaya had set the host in order and while the Bishop Don Hieronymo and Gil Diaz led away the body of the Cid, and Doña Ximena, and the baggage, he fell upon the Moors. First he attacked the tents of that Moorish Queen the Negress, who lay nearest to the city; and this onset was so sudden, that they killed full a hundred and fifty Moors before they had time to take arms or go to horse. But that Moorish Negress was so skilful in drawing the Turkish bow, that it was held for a marvel, and it is said that they called her in Arabic *Nugueymat Turya*, which is to say, the Star of the Archers. And she was the first that got on horseback, and with some fifty that were with her, did some hurt to the company of the Cid; but in fine they slew her, and her people fled to the camp. And so great was the uproar and confusion, that few there were who took arms, but instead thereof they turned their backs and fled toward the sea. And when King Bucar and his Kings saw this they were astonished. And it seemed to them that there came against them on the part of the Christians full seventy thousand knights, all as white as snow: and before them a knight of great stature upon a white horse with a bloody cross, who bore in one hand a white banner, and in the other a sword which seemed to be of fire, and he made a great mortality among the Moors who were flying. And King Bucar and the other Kings were so greatly dismayed that they never checked the reins till they had ridden into the sea; and the company of the Cid rode after them, smiting and slaying and giving them no respite; and they smote down so many that it was marvellous, for the Moors did not turn their heads to defend themselves. And when they came to the sea, so great was the press among them to get to the ships, that more than ten thousand died in the water. And of the six and thirty Kings, twenty and two were slain. And King Bucar and they who escaped with him hoisted sails and went their way, and never more turned their heads.

Bibliography

Many versions exist of the *Poema del Cid*. Those translations used in the preparation of this volume are as follows:

Hamilton, R. & Perry, J. *The Poem of the Cid* Penguin, London, 1984.

Merwin, W.S. *The Poem of the Cid* Dent, London, 1959.

Simpson, L.B. *The Poem of the Cid* University of California Press, 1957.

Southey, R. *Chronicle of the Cid* Routledge, London, 1883.

Other commentaries referred to included:

Arnoux, A. *La Legend du Cid Campeador* Club des Libraries de France, 1960.

Hook, D. 'The Conquest of Valencia' in *Cantar de mio Cid* pp120–26. Bulletin of Hispanic Studies, Vol. 50, 1973.

Merwin, W.S. *Some Spanish Ballads* Abelard Schumann, 1961.

Pidal, R.M. *The Cid & His Spain* (trans. Sunderland, H.), John Murray, London, 1934.

Spence, L. *Legends and Romances of Spain* Harrap, London, 1920.

Vilar, P. *Spain, A Brief History* Pergamon Press, Oxford, 1967.

GENEALOGY OF CHARACTERS

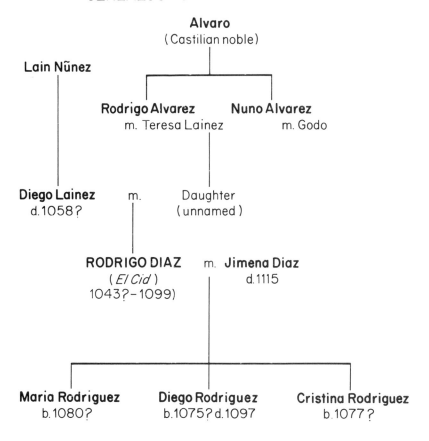

Alvaro
(Castilian noble)

Lain Nũnez

Rodrigo Alvarez
m. Teresa Lainez

Nuno Alvarez
m. Godo

Diego Lainez
d.1058?

m.

Daughter
(unnamed)

RODRIGO DIAZ
(*El Cid*)
1043?-1099)

m. **Jimena Diaz**
d.1115

Maria Rodriguez
b.1080?

Diego Rodriguez
b.1075? d.1097

Cristina Rodriguez
b.1077?

THE KINGS OF CASTILLE AND LEON

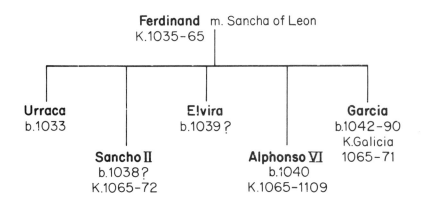

Ferdinand
K.1035-65

m. Sancha of Leon

Urraca
b.1033

Elvira
b.1039?

Garcia
b.1042-90
K.Galicia
1065-71

Sancho II
b.1038?
K.1065-72

Alphonso VI
b.1040
K.1065-1109

47

Index

Page numbers in *italics* refer to illustrations.

Illustrations

Colour plates by James Field.
Line illustrations by Chesca Potter.
Map and diagrams by Chartwell Illustrators.
Photographs and other illustrations courtesy of Peter Newark's Historical Pictures (pages 13 and 27) and Spanish National Tourist Board (pages 7, 11, 16, 25, 29 and 35).